RICE DIET MEAL PLAN RECIPES BOOK

The Rice Diet Revolution: How To Take Control Of Your Health And Create A Whole New You

IDRIS SAMSON

Contents

CHAPTER ONE

An Introductory

Rice, fruits, vegetables, and moderate amounts of lean protein make up the bulk of the low-fat, low-salt, low-calorie Rice Diet.

The diet's primary goals are to promote weight loss, lower blood pressure and cholesterol levels, and reduce inflammation. Some doctors now recommend modified versions of the Rice Diet to their patients as a means of improving their diet and losing weight, even though the original plan has been phased out.

Possible Gains And Losses

The Rice Diet may provide these health benefits:

• The Rice Diet is a low-calorie eating plan that may aid in weight loss. You can generate a calorie deficit and lose weight by switching to low-calorie items like fruits, vegetables, and rice and reducing your intake of high-calorie foods.

• The reduced salt and fat content of the Rice Diet have been shown to have a beneficial effect on blood pressure. People with high blood pressure will benefit greatly from this.

• The low-fat strategy of the Rice Diet can also help reduce cholesterol levels.

• Benefits for patients with type 2 diabetes include increased sensitivity to the hormone insulin due to eating a diet rich in complete grains like brown rice.

• The Rice Diet's high fiber content aids digestion and helps keep you regular.

Dangers Associated With A High-Rice Diet

• The Rice Diet is low in protein, calcium, and vitamin D, which might lead to deficiencies if followed for an extended period of time without the right supplements.

• The Rice Diet is difficult to stick to for any length of time due to its bland and restrictive nature. This may cause hunger and cause you to overeat.

• A lack of energy, especially at the outset, is a common side effect of low-calorie diets.

• The Rice Diet may not be appropriate for everyone, particularly those with certain health issues. Before beginning any new diet, it is recommended that you speak with a medical expert.

The Science Behind The Diet's Weight-Loss And Health Benefits

In a number of ways, the Rice Diet helps you lose weight and feel better:

• The Rice Diet is a calorie-restricted eating plan since it emphasizes eating less food. Because of this, you will be in a caloric deficit, which can aid in weight loss.

• The Rice Diet minimizes your intake of high-calorie and high-fat meals because of its low-fat nature. As a result, you may be able to cut back on calories and lose weight.

• The Rice Diet's emphasis on a low-sodium diet has been shown to have beneficial effects on blood pressure and cardiovascular health.

• The high fiber content of the Rice Diet makes you feel full for longer, cuts your appetite, and aids with digestion.

• The Rice Diet has an emphasis on eating entire foods, such as fruits, vegetables, and whole grains, which are packed with essential nutrients and relatively low in calories.

• Because of their high calorie, fat, and sodium content, processed foods are limited on the Rice Diet.

The Rice Diet is an approach of eating that emphasizes the consumption of nutrient-rich whole foods while discouraging the consumption of processed and high-fat foods. Individuals who adhere to the program report experiencing less inflammation, reduced blood pressure and cholesterol levels, and enhanced digestion as a result of the weight loss.

CHAPTER TWO

Permitted Foods For The Rice Diet

Foods that are low in fat, sodium, and calories are the focus of the Rice Diet. Some meals that are acceptable on the Rice Diet include:

• The Rice Diet calls for brown rice as its main source of carbohydrate. Nutritionally, it scores highly for fiber, vitamins, and minerals.

• Fruits: both fresh and frozen varieties of fruit are permitted on the Rice Diet. They contain little calories, lots of fiber, and beneficial nutrients.

• The Rice Diet permits an unlimited supply of veggies. They contain little calories, lots of fiber, and beneficial nutrients.

• The Rice Diet permits the use of legumes such as beans, lentils, and chickpeas. You can get some protein, fiber, and vitamins from them.

• Small amounts of lean protein are permitted on the Rice Diet and include things like skinless chicken, fish, and egg whites.

• Dairy items that are low in fat, such as skim milk, plain yogurt, and cottage cheese, are permitted on the Rice Diet. Among other nutrients, they include calcium and protein.

• Almonds, walnuts, and chia seeds, among others, are allowed in moderate quantities on the Rice Diet. They provide beneficial nutrients like fiber, protein, and healthy fats.

• Flavoring your Rice Diet meals with herbs and spices is allowed. They are a great addition because of their low calorie count and potential health advantages.

In general, foods high in nutrients and low in calories, fat, and sodium can be found throughout the Rice Diet. Individuals might enhance their health and lose weight by adhering to the diet.

Dietary Food Restrictions

High-calorie, high-fat, high-sodium, and high-added-sugar items are limited or eliminated on the Rice Diet. While on the Rice Diet, you should avoid these types of meals.

• Disallowed on the Rice Diet due to their high caloric and fat content are fried meals.

• Sodium, added sugars, and harmful fats are commonly found in processed foods such as packaged snacks, baked products, and canned foods. On the Rice Diet, they are strictly forbidden.

• High-fat meats: The Rice Diet prohibits fatty cuts of beef, hog, and lamb. They include a lot of sugar and unhealthy saturated fat.

• Dairy products with a high fat content are forbidden on the Rice Diet. This includes whole milk, cheese, and cream. They include a lot of sugar and unhealthy saturated fat.

• White bread, white pasta, and white rice are all off-limits on the Rice Diet because they are refined grains. They can cause a rapid rise in blood sugar since they are devoid of fiber and other nutrients.

• Candies, soft drinks, and sweets are forbidden on the Rice Diet because of the large amounts of added sugars they contain. They raise and lower blood sugar levels and are therefore unhealthy.

• Processed meats, canned soups, and frozen meals are examples of items high in sodium that are not allowed on the Rice Diet. They are associated with fluid retention and hypertension.

The Rice Diet is characterized by a preference for minimally processed, whole foods that are also low in calories, fat, and sodium. Weight loss and better health are both possible when people refrain from eating meals that are heavy in calories, fat, and salt.

CHAPTER THREE

Recipes And Menu Examples

Recipes and sample meal plans for the Rice Diet are provided below.

First Sample Menu:

Breakfast:

• Fresh berry and almond milk porridge made with brown rice.

• Herbal tea.

Snack:

• A snack with apple slices and almond butter.

Lunch:

- Vegetable and bean salad topped with grilled chicken breast.

- A sauce made of olive oil and balsamic vinegar.

Snack:

- Carrots with hummus on skewers.

Dinner:

- Garlic and lemon broccoli and green bean medley.

- Salmon fillet in the oven.

- Diced tomatoes and herbs atop a bed of brown rice pilaf.

Second Sample Menu:

Breakfast:

- Avocado and tomato on whole-grain toast.

- 100% Pure Orange Juice.

Snack:

- Low-fat Greek yogurt topped with strawberry slices.

Lunch:

- A salad of quinoa, black beans, and other greens.

- Dressing: Salsa.

Snack:

- A handful of raw almonds and an apple.

Dinner:

• Chicken breast marinated in lemon juice and rosemary, then grilled.

• Steamed asparagus.

• Pilaf of lentils and brown rice with roasted bell peppers.

Recipes for those on the Rice Diet can be found below.

1. Vegetable Stir Fry with Brown Rice

Ingredients:

• 1 cup of brown rice.

• 1 tbsp. of olive oil.

- One cup of veggies (carrots, peas, broccoli, etc.).

- 1 minced clove of garlic.

- 1 tbsp low-sodium soy sauce.

- Honey, 1 tsp.

- The right amount of salt and pepper.

Instructions:

- Prepare brown rice as directed on the package.

- Olive oil should be heated in a skillet over medium heat.

- For 5-7 minutes, sauté the garlic and mixed vegetables until the vegetables are soft.

- In a separate bowl, combine the soy sauce and honey.

- Once the rice is done cooking, add it to the skillet along with the soy sauce mixture and toss to blend.

- To taste, season with salt and pepper.

2. Salmon with Brown Rice Pilaf in the Oven

Ingredients:

For four people:

- 2) Olive oil, about a tablespoon.

- Dry Thyme, 1 tsp.

- A pinch of dried oregano.

- The right amount of salt and pepper.

- Brown rice, cooked to yield 2 cups.

- Diced tomatoes, half a cup.

- One-fortieth cup of chopped fresh parsley.

Instructions:

- Turn the oven temperature up to 375 degrees Fahrenheit.

- Prepare a baking sheet by lining it with parchment paper.

• Spread some olive oil on a baking sheet and sprinkle some thyme, oregano, salt, and pepper on salmon fillets.

• Cook salmon fillets in the oven for about 20 minutes, or until they are no longer raw in the center.

• Cooked brown rice, diced tomatoes, and chopped parsley should be combined in a medium bowl.

• Prepare a brown rice pilaf to accompany the salmon fillets.

Whole, nutrient-dense foods and easy, healthy cooking methods may make the Rice Diet delicious and filling.

CHAPTER FOUR

How To Buy For And Prepare Meals

Preparing meals and shopping for the week ahead can be useful parts of the Rice Diet because they increase the likelihood that people will have access to nutritious foods when they need them.

Prepare your Rice Diet meals and purchase more efficiently with these pointers.

• Take some time on Sunday to plan your meals for the week before you walk out to the store on Monday. In the long term, this can help you save both time and money by ensuring that you have everything you need.

• Create a list of the items you will need to get from the grocery store based on your meal plan. Make a list of what you need before you go shopping and stick to it.

• Focus your grocery store shopping on the outer aisles, where you will find more healthful options including fresh produce, lean meats, and low-fat dairy goods. Stay away from the middle aisles where you will find the bulk of the convenience meals and snacks.

• Stocking up on nutritious nutrients, including whole grains, nuts, and seeds, can be done on a budget by purchasing these items in large quantities.

• Plan ahead: On the weekends, make some of your meals and snacks for the coming week. Vegetables can be chopped, brown rice or quinoa can be cooked, and raw nuts and seeds can be portioned out.

• Purchase a variety of storage containers to facilitate meal planning and food organization. Glass containers are convenient since they can be used again and are safe to use in the microwave and dishwasher.

• Try out new herbs and spices, and get creative in the kitchen to make The Rice Diet tasty and fulfilling. Make your meals more exciting by incorporating new ingredients and techniques.

If you put in the time and effort up front, the Rice Diet can be a healthy and pleasurable approach to lose weight and enhance your overall well-being.

Adapting Your Way Of Life And Including Exercise

Incorporating regular exercise and making other lifestyle adjustments, in addition to following the Rice Diet, can significantly improve health and weight loss outcomes.

Some suggestions for making exercise and healthier habits part of your daily life:

• If you are just getting started with exercise or have not been active in a while, set modest, manageable objectives for yourself.

Some examples of this kind of activity are going for a daily stroll or spending 10 minutes each morning doing some light stretching.

• Exercise does not have to be chores if you find something you enjoy doing. Do something you enjoy doing every day, whether it is dancing, swimming, or playing a sport.

• Maintaining motivation and keeping tabs on progress is much easier if attainable goals are set. Consider scheduling 30-minute walks three times each week.

• Encouragement and accountability from loved ones can go a long way toward keeping you on track. Think about signing up for a fitness class or looking for a workout partner.

• Alter your routine: While exercise is essential for good health and weight loss, so are other, less strenuous modifications to your daily routine.

Reducing stress, getting enough sleep, not smoking, and not drinking too much are all examples of what can help.

• In order to see results from your exercise and other lifestyle modifications, you must be consistent. Make working out and other healthy behaviors a regular part of your life.

• Alternating between different types of exercise and other activities can protect you from becoming bored.

Alternate between cardio, strength training, and stretching to get the most out of your workouts.

The health benefits of the Rice Diet can be maximized by making other modifications to one's lifestyle, such as taking up regular exercise.

Always check in with your doctor before making any major changes to your diet, exercise routine, or medication.

CHAPTER FIVE

Typical Obstacles And Solutions

The Rice Diet, like any other eating plan, is not without its difficulties. Followers of the Rice Diet may have the following difficulties, as well as suggestions for resolving them:

• Eating the same items on a regular basis might get dull and trigger desires for bad options. To avoid this, play around with various herbs, spices, and seasonings to give your food more depth and diversity.

You should also try eating more fruits and vegetables and experimenting with different cuisines.

• Eating out at restaurants or going to parties can be difficult when you are trying to watch what you eat. To avoid these predicaments, think ahead and study the menu or offer to bring a nutritious food to share. Make good food and social choices and relax with friends and family.

• Some people struggle with emotional eating, which can be counterproductive to their weight loss goals. You can conquer emotional eating by learning what sets off your binges and using healthy coping mechanisms, like mindfulness or doing something that you enjoy.

• Keeping to a strict food plan while traveling might be challenging. Pack fresh fruits, raw nuts, and seeds as snacks, and study up on healthy dining options at your destination. Take advantage of your time away from home to get some exercise and fresh air.

• Challenges with diet compliance can stem from cravings for unhealthy foods. Eating nutrient-dense, full, and delicious foods can help you fight cravings. You can also try to recognize situations that set off your cravings so you can prepare a countermeasure, such as taking a walk or calling a friend.

• For some, the biggest obstacle to sticking to a healthy eating plan is a lack of drive. The best way to keep yourself motivated is to make a plan, stick to it, and reward yourself at key points along the way. You could also talk to close friends and relatives or get some help from a doctor.

Overall, the Rice Diet can be difficult, but it is possible to succeed with the appropriate approach and assistance.

Conclusion

Weight loss, better health markers, and a decreased risk of chronic diseases have all been associated with following the Rice Diet, which is low in salt, low in fat, and high in fiber.

Fruits, vegetables, whole grains, and legumes are highlighted on the diet, along with a restriction on processed foods, animal products, and added sugars. Some difficulties with the diet are inevitable, such as boredom with food options or social circumstances, but they may be handled.

The health advantages of the Rice Diet can be maximized by also adhering to a regimen of regular exercise and adopting other healthy lifestyle habits.

If you have any preexisting health conditions or take any medications, you should talk to your doctor before beginning any new diet or activity plan. The Rice Diet can be an effective tool for weight loss and general health improvement if followed correctly.

THE END

Made in the USA
Las Vegas, NV
28 January 2024

85014542R00024